SOMETIMES YOU JUST NEED TO GO TO ILLYRIA DISGUISED AS A PAGE BOY AND CAUSE CHAOS THAT DOUBLES WHEN YOUR TWIN SHOWS UP.

INSPIRED BY
TWELFTH NIGHT, WILLIAM SHAKESPEARE

THE WORST PART ABOUT AIR
TRAVEL IS WHEN YOU FLY TOO
CLOSE TO THE SUN ON WINGS
MADE OF WAX AND PLUMMET
INTO THE SEA AS A RESULT
OF YOUR OWN HUBRIS.

TRAVELING IS NICE, BUT COMING
HOME AND SLAUGHTERING
ALL THE SUITORS IN YOUR
FEAST ROOM IS BETTER.

INSPIRED BY
THE ODYSSEY, HOMER

ROAD TRIP RULES: PACK LIGHTLY. NO BACKSEAT DRIVING. WHOEVER SPOTS THE WHITE WHALE FIRST GETS THE GOLD COIN THAT'S AFFIXED TO THE MAINMAST. DON'T FORGET TO BRING SNACKS.

INSPIRED BY
MOBY-DICK, HERMAN MELVILLE

THE BEST PART ABOUT VISITING
NEW YORK CITY IN THE WINTERTIME
IS ASKING ALL THE CABDRIVERS
WHERE THE DUCKS GO.

INSPIRED BY
THE CATCHER IN THE RYE, J. D. SALINGER

IN SOLIDARITY WITH JANE
AUSTEN CHARACTERS, I, TOO,
WILL BE TAKING A SPA TRIP TO
BATH AND JUST HOPING IT WILL
SOLVE ALL MY PROBLEMS.

INSPIRED BY
VARIOUS JANE AUSTEN NOVELS

MY TRAVEL TIPS? TAKE A GUIDED TOUR. TRUST ME, YOU'LL APPRECIATE IT WHEN YOU'RE JOURNEYING THROUGH THE NINE CIRCLES OF HELL ACCOMPANIED BY THE POET VIRGIL.

INSPIRED BY
THE DIVINE COMEDY, DANTE ALIGHIERI

MUCH LIKE THE CURSED PAINTING
IN DORIAN GRAY'S ATTIC, MY
PASSPORT PHOTO SOMEHOW LOOKS
WORSE EVERY TIME I LOOK AT IT.

INSPIRED BY
THE PICTURE OF DORIAN GRAY, OSCAR WILDE

THE MOST INTERESTING THING
I'VE DONE DURING MY TRAVELS?
PROBABLY THE TIME I KILLED
AN OLD MAN AT A CROSSROADS,
BECAME KING OF THEBES,
AND ACCIDENTALLY MARRIED
MY MOM IN THE PROCESS.

INSPIRED BY
OEDIPUS REX, SOPHOCLES

I TRAVELED FROM OKLAHOMA
TO CALIFORNIA DURING THE DUST
BOWL AND ALL I GOT WAS THE
KNOWLEDGE THAT THE AMERICAN
DREAM IS UNATTAINABLE.

INSPIRED BY
THE GRAPES OF WRATH, JOHN STEINBECK

BACK IN MY DAY WE DIDN'T
HAVE PODCASTS. TO PASS THE
TIME WE'D HOLD STORYTELLING
CONTESTS DURING OUR
PILGRIMAGE TO CANTERBURY.

INSPIRED BY
THE CANTERBURY TALES, GEOFFREY CHAUCER

SORRY I DIDN'T RESPOND TO YOUR TEXT. I LEFT TOWN FOR FIVE YEARS TO EARN A FORTUNE IN BOOTLEGGING SO I COULD STARE AT THE GREEN LIGHT ACROSS THE WAY AND THROW PARTIES.

INSPIRED BY
THE GREAT GATSBY, F. SCOTT FITZGERALD

ALWAYS BRING A CONCH SHELL WITH YOU ON YOUR TRAVELS BECAUSE YOU NEVER KNOW WHEN YOU'RE GOING TO FIND YOURSELF STRANDED ON A DESERTED ISLAND WITH A BUNCH OF BRITISH CHOIRBOYS.

INSPIRED BY
LORD OF THE FLIES, WILLIAM GOLDING

SO WHEN DON QUIXOTE
JOURNEYS THROUGH THE
SPANISH COUNTRYSIDE AND TRIES
TO FIGHT A WINDMILL IT'S "A
LITERARY CLASSIC," BUT WHEN
I DO IT I'M "SCARING THE OTHER
PASSENGERS ON THE TOUR BUS."

INSPIRED BY
DON QUIXOTE, MIGUEL DE CERVANTES

THE BIGGEST MISTAKE YOU CAN
MAKE WHILE TRAVELING IS TAKING
A NAP ON THE FOREST FLOOR
AND FALLING VICTIM TO THE
WHIMS OF MISCHIEVOUS FAIRIES.

INSPIRED BY
A MIDSUMMER NIGHT'S DREAM, WILLIAM SHAKESPEARE

IF ANYONE NEEDS ME, I'LL BE
JOURNEYING TO THE CEDAR
FOREST IN ORDER TO SLAY
ITS GUARDIAN, HUMBABA.

INSPIRED BY
THE EPIC OF GILGAMESH, ANONYMOUS

TRAVELING IS MOSTLY JUST
GETTING LOST, WASHING ASHORE
ON THE COUNTRY ISLAND OF
LILLIPUT, AND BEING CHARGED
WITH TREASON BY PEOPLE WHO
ARE BARELY SIX INCHES TALL.

INSPIRED BY
GULLIVER'S TRAVELS, JONATHAN SWIFT

FOCUS ON THE JOURNEY,
NOT THE DESTINATION—
ESPECIALLY WHEN THE
DESTINATION IS SOMEWHERE
DEEP IN THE MONTRESOR
CATACOMBS, BRICKED UP IN A
CRYPT WITH NO SIGN OF WINE.

INSPIRED BY
"THE CASK OF AMONTILLADO," EDGAR ALLAN POE

STERLING
New York

An Imprint of Sterling Publishing Co., Inc.

STERLING and the distinctive Sterling logo
are registered trademarks of Sterling Publishing Co., Inc.

ISBN 978-1-4549-4488-1

Distributed in Canada by Sterling Publishing Co., Inc.
^{c}/o Canadian Manda Group, 664 Annette Street
Toronto, Ontario, Canada M6S 2C8
Distributed in the United Kingdom by GMC Distribution Services
Castle Place, 166 High Street, Lewes, East Sussex, England BN7 1XU
Distributed in Australia by NewSouth Books
University of New South Wales, Sydney, NSW 2052, Australia

For information about custom editions, special sales,
and premium and corporate purchases, please contact
Sterling Special Sales at 800-805-5489 or
specialsales@sterlingpublishing.com.

Manufactured in India

2 4 6 8 10 9 7 5 3 1

sterlingpublishing.com

Text by Courtney Gorter
Design by Christine Heun
Cover by Melissa Farris